The Success Mindset

Eliminating Self-Doubt

Louistas Nyuyse

Copyright © 2022 Louistas Nyuyse

All rights reserved. No part of this publication may be reproduced, distributed, or transmitted in any form or by any means, including photocopying, recording, or any other electronic or mechanical methods, without the prior written permission of the publisher, except in the case of brief quotations embodied in critical reviews and certain other noncommercial uses permitted by copyright law. For permission, write to the publisher at:

Greatness University Publishers
London, UK
www.greatnessuniversity.co.uk

ISBN: 978-1-913164-18-8
ISBN-13: 978-1-913164-18-8

The Success Mindset©

LOUISTAS NYUYSE

Also, Author of **Think Like a VIRUS:** *The C.O.R.O.N.A. Effect*

CONTENTS

Introduction	1
Chapter 1: What is Self-Doubt	5
Chapter 2: Why Do We Doubt Ourselves?	23
Chapter 3: Break the Cycle	51
Chapter 4: Further Tips and Articles on How to Multiply Your Self-Confidence	117
Chapter 5: How to Overcome Self-Doubt when Presenting Ideas to Your Peers	127
Chapter 6: Self-Assertiveness Strategies to Help You Reclaim Your Domain	135
Chapter 7: I Can, I Will, I Must Be Confident	147
Conclusion	165

ACKNOWLEDGMENTS

Success is interdependence and the successful mindset depends on meaningful interdependence.

This work is a product of many souls. It started with my decision to go against the norm of "obeying your superiors without questioning in 2002". Disobedience to authority figures who made decisions against my will cast doubts on my own judgments. And subsequently led to self-doubt, low self-esteem, and fear of independence and progress.

But I am grateful for the inspiration from spiritual books, like The Jerusalem Bible, the motivation from great speakers and the wisdom shared by so many over the modern social media.

I am grateful for the works of Norman Vincent Peale, Robert Kiyosaki, Napoleon Hill, Franklin Convey, Jeff Olson, Bernard Roth, Dale Carnegie, Jack Cranfield, Neale Donald Walsch, Timothy Ferriss and more. I am also grateful to speakers whose trainings I have attended and found great content to awake my soul like Tony Robbins, Les Brown, Forbes Riley, and Success Resources for further exposing me to their various coaches and mentors, to whom my future career now "remembers".

Through deep reflection on newly gained knowledge and the Re-membering of my childhood consciousness, I have synchronized some of the information that helped me to overcome self-doubt and develop confidence in sharing this knowledge.

Discussions in all my mastermind groups have assisted me so much to reshape the knowledge I have gained and form my own opinions. I thank all my colleagues for their wisdom.

It has been long nights of studying and writing away from family and I thank my family immensely for their love, understanding, and support.

Finally, my gratitude goes to The Greatness University Publishers for their generosity in publishing this work and making it available to you. Through them, more shall become confident and successful from these pages.

Final thanks to you for reading this book and through it I now know you.

Introduction

I Can, I Will, I must!

The Success Mindset

Everyone doubts themselves. I'm sure you can think of many occasions when you second guessed what you were doing or told yourself that there was no way you could do what you wish you could.

In other words, self-doubt is a normal part of being human. What matters is how you respond to that little voice in your head that whispers *"It can't be done"*. You have two choices when it comes to responding to that voice. You can heed it, or you can go on and do something anyway.

How you respond to self-doubt affects all areas of your live. It affects your personal life, your happiness, your relationships, work, finances, family etc. That's why it's so important to learn more about self-doubt and how to respond to it. By taking control, we can shape our life the way we would like it to be.

And that's what this guide is all about. We'll start by talking about what exactly self-doubt is and what effect it can have on our lives.

Next, we'll cover some of the reasons why we doubt ourselves in the first place, and finally wrap it all up by figuring out how we can break out of this cycle of self-doubt. After all what good would a guide about self-doubt be without some hands-on tools for taking control and

The Success Mindset

banishing that little voice in your head.

My hope is that you find this guide helpful in learning more about self-doubt, recognizing when you're doubting yourself, and then finding a way for you to deal with it that helps you reach your goals, whatever they may be. I'm not promising it will be easy, but I do promise to provide you with the tools you need to accomplish this. Let's start by taking a closer look at what exactly self-doubt is and what it can do to you and your life.

Connect with Louistas

The Success Mindset

[Connect with Louistas](#)

Chapter 1

What Is Self-Doubt?

How You See One Thing Is How You See Everything!

[Connect with Louistas](#)

The Success Mindset

Self-doubt is the "lack of confidence in oneself and one's abilities." In other words, when you doubt yourself, you don't feel confident in what you're trying to do or accomplish. And that's a big problem.

Self-doubt is that little voice in the back of your head that constantly tells you that you're not going to reach your goals, that you're not doing things right, and that you should just stop right now since you're not accomplishing anything anyway. It's a way to protect ourselves from disappointment. When we set the bar low and don't expect to do well, we won't be disappointed when we don't reach our lofty goals. Or even worse, it's what makes us give up before we even start – while convincing us that it's in our best interest.

Sadly, that doesn't push us to go further, reach higher, and get more done. Instead that little voice of self-doubt keeps us in a place where we're comfortable. It keeps us at a level where we're doing the bare minimum to stay where we're at. And I don't have to tell you that this doesn't allow for much growth no matter what area of your life you're dealing with – be it your personal life, your business, your job, your relationships, your hobbies, or anything else.

Connect with Louistas

Instead, growth and success occur when we step outside of that comfort zone, do the stuff that scares us, and stretch ourselves to do more than we thought we were capable of. But when we let self-doubt get the better of us – day in and day out – that's not going to happen, is it? And remember, how you see one thing, is how you see everything. When you get into this cycle, your view of self, others and things just remains the same.

And that can have some detrimental effects on all aspects of our lives. It's normal to want to grow and better yourself. Not being able to do so because of self-doubt can send you down a spiral of feeling worthless, getting depressed, and as a result even more self-doubt since you are continually proving yourself right. It's a vicious cycle and it takes some time and effort to break it… but break it you can and that's what this guide is about.

Before we dive into the next chapter and talk in more detail about why we doubt ourselves and get to the root of things, let's look at how self-doubt can have a negative effect on every aspect of your live.

Connect with Louistas

The Success Mindset

You Challenge

What Areas in your life has doubt set in?

Name it! Conquer it!

Physical?

....
....
....
....
....
....
....
....
....
....
....
....
....
....
....

Connect with Louistas

Spiritual?

Emotional?

[Connect with Louistas](#)

Psychological?

Social?

Connect with Louistas

How Self-Doubt Affects Your Personal Life and Relationships

Self-doubt can have a profound negative affect on your personal life. It can keep you from meeting new people that will enrich your life. It can keep you from deepening relationships and friendships because you are afraid to open up.

Relationships are two-way streets. You need to be open, vulnerable, and go out there and communicate. If you are afraid to mess up, or get turned down, you risk missing out on new friends and maybe even that significant other.

Confidence is contagious and we're attracted to people that seem to know what they are doing and who are putting themselves out there. Self-doubt keeps us from developing that self-confidence and the chance of making connections and building relationships with those around us.

Self-doubt can even affect your health. Lack of confidence and happiness can lead to anything from depression to anxiety and with-it high blood pressure, which isn't good for the health of your heart, for example.

Connect with Louistas

The Success Mindset

Your Notes! Your Symptoms

....

....

....

....

....

....

....

....

....

....

....

....

....

....

....

....

....

....

[Connect with Louistas](#)

[Connect with Louistas](#)

How Self-Doubt Affects Your Work and Your Professional Life

Doubting yourself can also negatively impact your career and your livelihood. Who do you think is more likely to get the new job or the promotion? The person who presents themselves in a confident and self-assured manner, or the doubter?

Of course, it's the confident person. And it's not just during interviews and job evaluations that self-doubt will hurt you. It makes it harder to do your everyday job. It's not fun to second guess yourself with everything you do.

Work will go faster, smoother, and be better if you're confident in what you are doing. That's why it is so important to focus on banishing self-doubt and boosting confidence. You'll be happier and better paid in the end.

Your professional life would be more colorful, rewarding, and influential the more you become confident. They say that confidence is infectious. And the infectious ones sometimes offer more value to society since people look up to them as models, heroes and pacesetters. The hero lives in you, being crippled by self-doubt. And your profession needs you to awaken the giant in you and save those who are also trapped by this demon – self-doubt.

[Connect with Louistas](#)

The Success Mindset

Your Notes! Your Symptoms!

....

....

....

....

....

....

....

....

....

....

....

....

....

....

....

....

....

....

....

Connect with Louistas

The Success Mindset

[Connect with Louistas](#)

How Self-Doubt Affects Your Finances and Possessions

Let's go back to those job offers and promotions you're missing out on. How much less money are you making for years and years to come because you missed just one promotion, or didn't get the job offer you wanted and had to settle for something that paid less?

It's hard to guess, but it could easily cost you a couple of hundred bucks per week. And that's just one promotion you didn't get. It doesn't stop there. Since you didn't get that promotion, you also won't make it up to the next level that pays even better and has better benefits and so forth. Over the course of your career, self-doubt could cost you hundreds of thousands of dollars.

And that kind of money can have a huge impact on your family. Without the extra income, you may be struggling to pay the bills each month. That may cause your credit score to go down and as result you'll be paying more for the car and house you're buying because you'll end up with a higher interest rate.

It also means that you have to settle for a used car and a much smaller house than you'd hoped to buy. And let's not forget about all the fun little extras like going out to

Connect with Louistas

eat, taking your wife and kids shopping, or heading out on a fun family trip twice a year. That's not going to be possible when you're just scraping by.

Instead, you're living frugally, cutting corners where you can, and staying up at night worrying about money. That doesn't sound like a good life, does it?

The more you sink low into poverty, you develop a poverty mindset. Then the wealthy mindset flies out of the window. Your acquaintances and friends become the same people with less wealth, fewer possessions, no savings with increased debtors and more bills to pay. And self-doubt loves this form of existence; it feeds on it and brings in brother low self-esteem, cousin depression and then unemployment. But the good news is that you, you can stop this vicious family right on its track.

To recap, self-doubt makes you feel less confident in your abilities to accomplish things and that can have quite the negative effect on every part of your life. But thankfully the reverse is true as well. As you start to get things done, your confidence goes up and your self-doubt goes down.

Before we dig deeper into how we can break out of this vicious cycle of self-doubt, let's take a closer look at what causes it in the next chapter.

Connect with Louistas

The Success Mindset

Your Notes! Your Symptoms!

....

....

....

....

....

....

....

....

....

....

....

....

....

....

....

....

....

....

....

[Connect with Louistas](#)

[Connect with Louistas](#)

Chapter 2

Why Do We Doubt Ourselves?

If You Believe You Can, You Can!

If You Believe You Can't, You Probably Can't!

Connect with Louistas

There are a lot of different reasons why we may doubt ourselves. Some may seem valid, others not so much. But in either case we don't stand a chance of overcoming these self-doubts if we don't acknowledge them first and then come up with a plan for overcoming them. This chapter is dedicated to the first part. Let's start by taking a look at eight common reasons why we doubt ourselves.

We Don't Have The Know-How

Self-doubt can be caused by not knowing everything there is to know about a job, a task, a person, or a field. It would be great if we could know it all, but chances are that's not going to happen. And the doubt starts to creep up. You may be thinking about different scenarios that you don't feel prepared for, or you're thinking about all the people you know who you think would be much better qualified.

It's very normal to doubt yourself. What you do about it is what counts. And here's the important information to take away. Everyone doubts their skills and know-how. Some are just better at hiding those doubts and doing it anyway than others. The good news is that by reading these pages, you are now better off than many out there who may be consumed by this "I don't know-how syndrome". You are in the right place at the right time.

[Connect with Louistas](#)

The Success Mindset

Your Notes! Your Symptoms!

....

....

....

....

....

....

....

....

....

....

....

....

....

....

....

....

....

....

....

[Connect with Louistas](#)

[Connect with Louistas](#)

We Don't Know What To Expect

Another big reason for self-doubt to creep up is fear of the unknown. When you're meeting a new person or taking a new job, you can't possibly know everything about it. There are a lot of unknowns and that makes us uncomfortable or even fearful. And that fear turns into self-doubt. If we don't think we can do it and don't put ourselves out there, we don't have to face those unknowns.

When you see someone, you think you are falling in love with, you do not honestly know what to expect. When you give birth to a child, their destiny is entirely undetectable. When you sit in your car to drive, you only trust that it will take you to your desired location. When you eat food, you do not know that it will turn you into. But sometimes we take these things to heart, and they stop us from taking a leap. We stall because we are not sure of what is to come next.

The truth is that there is no possible way to know everything that's going to happen on a job, with a project, or in a relationship. Yes, we can prepare, but there will always be unknowns. The key is to find a way to say yes anyway and figure it out as you go along; to take the first step without asking how the next step shall be taken.

[Connect with Louistas](#)

The Success Mindset

Your Notes! Your Symptoms!

....
....
....
....
....
....
....
....
....
....
....
....
....
....
....
....
....
....
....

Connect with Louistas

Connect with Louistas

Our Past Catches Up With Us

It would be great if we all had perfect lives with no problems or issues. But that's just not the case. We all come with our own history and our own baggage. And some of those past experiences make us doubt ourselves and our abilities. Maybe it's a failed relationship that makes us think we're just not cut out for a long-term commitment like marriage. Maybe it's an incident with a boss or co-worker in a past job that makes us hesitant to try out for the promotion. Or maybe it's something completely different.

My very good science teacher was replaced by a young graduate who complicated our science learning process. I arrogantly decided to abandon sciences in preference of art. And now I am having a serious challenge re-learning the science I should have learnt in secondary school. The arrogance is catching up on me now. But should I let it consume me further?

We all have a past and that past leaves scars. Some are deeper than others, but they can all undermine our self-confidence and lead to self-doubt. Realizing that is the first step towards overcoming that doubt and with it our bad past with all its baggage.

Connect with Louistas

[Connect with Louistas](#)

The Success Mindset

Your Notes! Your Symptoms!

....
....
....
....
....
....
....
....
....
....
....
....
....
....
....
....
....
....

[Connect with Louistas](#)

[Connect with Louistas](#)

We've Been Told We Can't Do This

We are social creatures, brought up in a social environment – also known as a family. And from an early age, we've learned to listen to what those around us have to say. In particular we're paying attention to our parents, parent figures, mentors, teachers, and people of authority. We've learned to listen to them and heed their advice. We even listen to and act upon unconsciously picked up concepts, manners, and laws.

In early education, we were taught how to say no to this or no to that – starting from classroom rules to traffic laws, table manners to our religious laws, the will of the politicians and the unconscious amalgamation of these into one massive law in our own subconscious.

Hence, it's only natural to doubt ourselves and our decisions when one of those people we look up to, tells us that we can't do it. Sometimes the advice is sound. Sometimes it's self-serving. The key is to learn the difference and realize that part of growing up involves trying things, even when our "elders" advice against it; even when "society" thinks differently about it; and even when everyone does things differently. They aren't always right. You have also got an answer in you!

Connect with Louistas

The Success Mindset

Your Notes! Your Symptoms!

....
....
....
....
....
....
....
....
....
....
....
....
....
....
....
....
....
....

Connect with Louistas

[Connect with Louistas](#)

We Are Fearful

Sometimes we're just plain scared. We're afraid of the unknown, we're afraid to mess up, and we're afraid to find out that we aren't good enough. Fear is a strong motivator, and, in this case, fear causes self-doubt and motivates in-action.

Sooner or later, we settle for second best options. And the fear grows even stronger. And if we do not address it positively, fear convinces us that it does not exist and hence we wear a mask, believing we are all ok when we avoid those things we were scared of. And the consequences can be devastating.

So, we don't apply for our dream job, we don't go out and get that college education, we don't put our name in the hat for the promotion and we don't go talk to the cute girl or boy at the bar. All for fear of being let down. But guess what? When we let that fear rule us, we lose any chance we had for positive change. Isn't it worth doing something despite the fear, if we have a chance of getting what we really want?

When people overcome their fears, they look back and wonder why they were scared of illusions.

[Connect with Louistas](#)

The Success Mindset

Your Notes! Your Symptoms!

....
....
....
....
....
....
....
....
....
....
....
....
....
....
....
....
....
....
....

[Connect with Louistas](#)

The Success Mindset

[Connect with Louistas](#)

We Lack Self Esteem

We already talked about how self-doubt is a lack of confidence in our ability to get something done. It's also closely related to a lack of self-esteem. The two usually go hand in hand. We don't think we're good enough and we don't think we have what it takes – lack of self-esteem and lack of confidence. The end result is a double dose of self-doubt.

I once taught a student in secondary school who considered herself less intelligent than others. When she wrote the GCSE after great encouragement and counselling, the results came out and she would not touch the envelop to see her results. She burst out crying because she was convinced, she had failed. She kept the envelope sealed for three days and finally the younger brother secretly opened it. When he read the positive results at the dinner table that evening, the spell was broken. She is one confident solicitor now.

The good news is that as you work on banishing self-doubt, your self-esteem will go up and vice versa. And that self-esteem will help you banish more self-doubt. It's a self-propelling cycle. All you need to do is get the ball rolling. We'll talk about **how** in the next chapter.

Connect with Louistas

The Success Mindset

Your Notes! Your Symptoms!

....
....
....
....
....
....
....
....
....
....
....
....
....
....
....
....
....
....
....

Connect with Louistas

Connect with Louistas

We Don't Think We're Good Enough Yet

Another big issue that causes self-doubt is thinking that we don't know enough yet, or that we aren't experienced enough yet for a task, a job, or a position. That's a very normal feeling and to be honest, chances are when you take a new job or try something new, that you're not good at it. That's because you haven't tried it yet and you're lacking the experience, which usually comes with time.

Paul was a warehouse operator who assisted drivers to load products into the trucks. He did this job for years and observed how other colleagues were using folk lifts to do the job faster. He then learnt to use it. But in his mind, he convinced himself that he did not know much about the use of folk lifts. Although other colleagues saw him practice confidently, Paul still had this self-doubt about his operation skills. A job of a folk lift operator became available in the warehouse. As a matter of procedure, everyone had to be officially tested and certified for use. Paul was reminded by his line manager that he was the next best person for that job. Paul took the test and was unsuccessful. When he shared this story with me, my question to him was, "Do you know how to operate a folk lift?" His answer was an affirmative resounding "Yes!"

Connect with Louistas

The Success Mindset

And so, I asked, what happened? Paul said he did not think he knew enough and needed more practice. Someone else got the job and got a pay rise. Paul is the one supervising this new learner how to maneuver the folk lift from the side, with a smaller salary. Self-doubt killed his skills and ruined his promotion.

However, it's sometimes normal to doubt if you can do something. The important part is to try things anyway, get some experience under your belt, and get better at what you're doing. Think back to the first few weeks at your latest job.

Chances are that it was hard, and overwhelming, and that you didn't know how to do half the stuff you were suddenly responsible for. And you made it through those stress-full first few weeks. You got better at your job and eventually it became routine – something you could do in your sleep. If you drive now, the chances are that you are better than your first day. Do you remember that first day you took control of the steering wheel? And now, maybe you drive to your destination without even thinking about what you are doing – becoming an expert driver with time. The same goes for learning your favorite hobby. It takes time and it's ok to do stuff long before you know everything there is to know… which by the way isn't possible, no matter how well you prepare.

Connect with Louistas

The Success Mindset

Your Notes! Your Symptoms!

....
....
....
....
....
....
....
....
....
....
....
....
....
....
....
....
....
....
....

[Connect with Louistas](#)

[Connect with Louistas](#)

We're More Comfortable Where We're At Right Now

This next reason for self-doubt is closely related to the last one. Let's go back to the new job example. Yes, in the beginning it was hard and challenging. There was much you didn't know and a lot you had to figure out. Now though, that same job has become routine. It's fairly easy and you know what to do. You're comfortable doing what you're doing and that may be what's keeping you from applying for that promotion, using self-doubt as an excuse to keep you comfortable.

You have a choice to make. Will you stay comfortable where you're at, or are you ready to get a bit uncomfortable, face your fears, and face the unknown? As nice as it is to stay comfortable, it'll eventually get boring.

Are these the only reasons why we may doubt ourselves? Of course not. We each come from different backgrounds and have lived very different lives. As a result, we've developed self-doubt for different reasons. The ones listed above, are however some of the more common ones. And while they may not describe you and your circumstances perfectly, they should give you a good idea of where your self-doubt is coming from. And with that

Connect with Louistas

information, you can start to work towards silencing that self-doubt and listening to your confident voice instead. That part we'll tackle in the next chapter.

Your Notes! Your Symptoms!

....

....

....

....

....

....

....

....

....

....

....

....

....

....

....

....

Connect with Louistas

The Success Mindset

[Connect with Louistas](#)

The Success Mindset

Connect with Louistas

Chapter 3

Break The Cycle

Be The First Person To Participate

In Your Own Rescue!

Connect with Louistas

So far, we've talked extensively about what self-doubt is, what causes it, and how it can affect every single aspect of your life. I shared a few hints here and there on what you can do to overcome this feeling of doubt, but frankly, little tips here and there aren't enough.

Self-doubt can be a vicious, self-propelling cycle. But the good news is that it can be broken – it starts with you! All it takes is a little mind shift and then tricking yourself into doing things anyway. Yes, that's easier said than done, but I promise to give you all kinds of different tools and strategies to make it happen.

As much as I wish there was a simple step-by-step solution to getting rid of self-doubt, there isn't. And if you think about it for a minute, it makes sense. We all live different lives, have different experiences, and with that, have different things that make us doubt ourselves. When you read through the examples of things that can cause self-doubt in the last chapter, some probably resonated much more with you than others.

That's why there isn't a "one-size-fits-all" strategy for banishing self-doubt. And as such the solution will have to be custom tailored to you as well. Have no fear (or self-doubt), you'll find everything you need to get started in this chapter. Much like the last one, it is broken up into

Connect with Louistas

sections. Each of them will describe a different strategy to boost your confidence and lower your self-doubt. The first four tips are universal. Start there and implement them as quickly and as often as possible until they become second nature.

As for the rest, start with the ones that resonate with you the most. Incorporate those in your daily life and as they become habits, come back, and pick out something else to try. Rinse and repeat until you've silenced that little voice in your head that tells you that you aren't good enough or can't do this. Ready to get started on proving that little voice of self-doubt wrong?

And by the way, remember that there is a course that accompanies this book. You might had bought this book through the course or may be still to encounter the video course with more practical expressions of many concepts from this book. There is also a workbook designed to help you map out the tips that resonate with you and put action plans on how to implement and accomplish them. *"The Success Mindset Workbook: Eliminating Self-Doubt"* is a great resource for your growth, sustenance, and cultivation of confidence. Using these resources together will lift you so high that people will see your confidence when you walk into a room. Let's see how to achieve this.

Connect with Louistas

The Success Mindset

Your Notes! Your Symptoms!

How Committed are you to banish self-doubt?
How does it make you feel?

....

....

....

....

....

....

....

....

....

....

....

....

....

....

....

....

Connect with Louistas

[Connect with Louistas](#)

Make Yourself Do It Anyway

Let's start with something that sounds easy but is incredibly powerful. Whenever you feel yourself doubting that you can do something, do it anyway. You don't have to commit 100% all the time but get in the habit of at least giving things a try before you admit defeat.

For example, let's say you've had this dream of writing a novel, but you keep telling yourself that you'd never finish it, you aren't a good enough writer, and that even if you did manage to write it all, there's no way you could get it published. And even if you did, no one would want to buy it. Sound familiar?

Making yourself do it anyway in this example may mean taking a long weekend, or even a couple of weeks to write a short story, an essay, or a poem. Do the writing but on a smaller, more manageable, and less scary scale. Proof to yourself that you can get some pretty good writing done.

And with that confidence under your belt, you may just be brave enough to show the story to a few good friends or a fellow writer and get some feedback.

Before you know it, by just getting in the habit of trying

Connect with Louistas

The Success Mindset

something despite the self-doubt, you'll be tackling new things in all areas of your life that you never thought you would. It's a great habit to get into.

Your Notes! Your Symptoms!

What concrete action will you take?

....
....
....
....
....
....
....
....
....
....
....
....
....
....

Connect with Louistas

The Success Mindset

You're your fears!

The Success Mindset

Connect with Louistas

Ask Yourself "What's The Worst That Can Happen?"

But what if you try to make yourself do something scary like submitting that same short story for publication and just can't bring yourself to do it? What do you do when the voice of self-doubt is screaming at the top of its non-existent lungs?

You ask yourself this: "What's the worst that can happen?"

I'm serious. Ask yourself what the worst possible negative outcome could be. In other words, face your worst fear before you simply let self-doubt take over. In the example we used in the last section, ask yourself what's the worst that can happen if I submit my short story to a magazine, blog, or publisher? The worst that can happen is that they decline to publish it. And when you think about it, that's not that big of a deal. You can always submit it somewhere else or edit it and resubmit it down the road.

The joy here is that even if it was not published, you then had the opportunity to work on it and make it even better. He who does not fail has not tried hard enough, and she who fails, learns the lesson, and improves.

[Connect with Louistas](#)

Let's run through a few more examples:

Talking to the new girl at the bar or the new boy in town at the show – what's the worst that can happen? She's not interested, he's already taken. Hey, at least you tried.

Applying for the open management position at work – what's the worst that can happen? You don't get the job and you're exactly where you're at right now. Nothing gained, but also nothing lost. Might as well try.

When you ask yourself this one little question, the general feeling of fear and doubt vanishes. Instead, you're making yourself face the worst possible outcome and it's usually not nearly as bad as you think. Use this strategy to help yourself face the fear and doubt and then go do it anyway as suggested in the first tip.

The more you practice both of these techniques the easier it will become and the faster your self-doubt will vanish. If you don't take away anything else from this book, I hope you remember and use these two simple little strategies.

Think of one thing which you have put aside for a long time now and make a plan to use these strategies on it to start a process of confidence building and success. Use the following questions to assist you too in other areas.

Connect with Louistas

The Success Mindset

Your Notes! Your Symptoms!

What's the worst thing that can happen?

………………………………………………………………………………

………………………………………………………………………………

………………………………………………………………………………

………………………………………………………………………………

………………………………………………………………………………

………………………………………………………………………………

………………………………………………………………………………

………………………………………………………………………………

………………………………………………………………………………

………………………………………………………………………………

………………………………………………………………………………

………………………………………………………………………………

………………………………………………………………………………

………………………………………………………………………………

………………………………………………………………………………

………………………………………………………………………………

Connect with Louistas

What's the best thing that can happen?

Connect with Louistas

[Connect with Louistas](#)

Take Baby Steps

We talked about self-doubt and confidence. Your confidence in your own abilities can quickly vanish when you're looking at a huge task or face a big challenge. Let's go back to the writing and publishing the next great American novel or African fiction, example. That's a pretty daunting task. No wonder we doubt we can do it. Or how about wanting to restore a '57 Chevrolet that you found rusting away in an old barn? It's again completely normal to doubt yourself when you're looking at a huge project like that. Instead of trying to do it all at once and focusing on everything that needs doing, break it down into baby steps.

For the novel, focus on one little part of writing, like the plot or character development, or even just writing one scene. With the car, think about the first thing you need or can do. Get it home to your own garage for example. Next, you may want to start to assess damage and work on a list of things you need to repair. From there focus on one thing on that list and get that done.

Before you know it you're making some serious progress by taking one little baby step at a time. And since these little steps don't seem as difficult or complicated as the

Connect with Louistas

entire project, your self-doubt goes down and with each step completed your confidence goes up.

Your Notes! Your Symptoms!

Step No 1.

....
....
....
....
....
....
....

Step No 2.

....
....
....
....
....
....
....

Connect with Louistas

The Success Mindset

[Connect with Louistas](#)

Celebrate Small Successes

As you complete each baby step or reach small milestones along the way, take the time to celebrate your successes. Acknowledge that you're making progress and getting things done. You don't have to go out and buy a cake or host a big party. But make sure you realize how far you've come and what progress you've made.

Why is it important, you may ask? Because as you celebrate your success, no matter how small, you're building confidence and we've already established that confidence is the perfect antidote to self-doubt. So, pat yourself on the back and revel in your progress.

Easy ways of recognizing your progress are through the use of a journal - see *"The Success Mindset Workbook."* You could also use a post-it-note board-of-fame. When you achieve some success, write it down on a post-it note, and paste it on that board. Time and again, visit that board and imprint into your subconscious the fact that you have once conquered that issue. Also talk to people about what you do and how you have overcome the challenges - when people know that you are good at something, you also live by the truth they now know. It helps you become an expert, and builds your confidence.

Connect with Louistas

Your Notes! Your Symptoms!

Count your successes and name them here! Life, job, relationship, skills, studies!

....
....
....
....
....
....
....
....
....
....
....
....
....
....
....
....
....

[Connect with Louistas](#)

[Connect with Louistas](#)

Focus On Who You're Helping

Here's another powerful strategy for you to try. This works particularly well whenever you're feeling that you're not good enough. Instead of focusing on yourself and your level of expertise (or lack thereof), focus instead on who you are helping.

How would what you're thinking of doing help out others? Let's say you've been toying with the idea of teaching a class on keeping a personal budget. You've been budgeting for a while and used it as a tool to help you get out of debt. But you're no Dave Ramsey, so what business do you have teaching this?

Here's the thing Dave Ramsey isn't for everyone, and you may be reaching people that never heard of him, but desperately need help to get their personal finances under control. You're doing them a disservice by not teaching the class.

Focus on the clients or students you'll be helping with your class... or whatever it is you're thinking of doing. Think about the difference you'll make in their lives. Focus on that and your self-doubt will start to melt away. Try it – it works!

Connect with Louistas

The Success Mindset

Your Notes! Your Symptoms!

Who is it you are helping, You or others?

....

....

....

....

....

....

....

....

....

....

....

....

....

....

....

....

....

[Connect with Louistas](#)

[Connect with Louistas](#)

The Success Mindset

Find A Mentor, Mastermind Group, Or Accountability Partner

I'll let you in on a secret. You don't have to go it alone. It's hard and scary to start a new venture or business, or a new chapter in your life by yourself. Instead of playing lone wolf and figuring out everything the hard way, find a mentor, a mastermind or support group, or just a friend or college in a similar situation that can become your accountability partner.

As I was completing this book, I was attending a three mastermind groups. One was run by Forbes Riley called GSD – "Get Shit Done". Weekly we met to make sure that the weeks writing tasks were done. We got stuff done!

Having someone else there to talk to, to encourage and support you, and to answer questions can make a world of difference. Simply not being alone in this helps. As an added bonus you have someone there with you to tell you you're nuts when self-doubt starts to raise its ugly head. These people can be your very own personal cheerleaders that will lift you up and boost your esteem and confidence. And with that you may be ready to tackle some projects, tasks, and challenges that you thought were unattainable. Do you have accountability partners?

Connect with Louistas

Your Notes! Your Symptoms!

Mentors:

....
....
....
....
....
....
....
....

Groups:

....
....
....
....
....
....
....
....

Connect with Louistas

Accountability Partner:

....

....

....

....

....

....

....

....

....

Networks:

....

....

....

....

....

....

....

....

Connect with Louistas

The Success Mindset

Coach:

....
....
....
....
....
....
....
....
....
....
....
....
....
....
....
....
....
....
....
....

[Connect with Louistas](#)

The Success Mindset

[Connect with Louistas](#)

Create A "Feel Good" File

Here's a cold, hard truth. We all have bad days. We all have days when we doubt everything we do and are ready to throw in the towel. We have them as parents, we have them in our jobs, we have them in our marriage, and we have them as business owners. It happens and it's part of life. The key is to get out of that funk as quickly as possible, boost our confidence, and get back to work.

And there's a sneaky little trick to help us do that. I call it the "Feel Good" File. This can be a shoebox or a special folder on your computer. It doesn't matter where you keep it, just set it up so it's there when you have "one of those days".

In this file, or box, or where-ever you want to, put things that fill you with pride and confidence. It could be the picture your daughter drew of the two of you. It could be the email you got from your boss that praised your work on a project. It could be a heartfelt testimonial or thank you card from a client or customer. It could be a copy of the comment someone left on your social media profile that tugged your heart strings. It doesn't matter what it is and what's meaningful to me will be different from what's meaningful to you. But start collecting these little

[Connect with Louistas](#)

mementoes of moments when you felt so proud and confident that you thought you could reach the moon.

Stick them in a folder or a box and pull them out whenever you feel down, tired, and beaten down. They will remind you of better days and more importantly that no matter what happened today, what you do matters and that you are making a difference.

Do you have any certificates of achievement in the past? Do you know where they have been buried? Dig them out and display them. You have probably forgotten that you have those skills. Seeing your certificates imprints into your subconscious the confidence you had at the time of the achievement. Make it a duty to clean and enjoy them. That good feeling will defeat self-doubt and build confidence. Do you wonder why soldiers have to clean and shine their boots every day? It instills discipline, confidence, and order.

Are you an expert in anything – it does not matter what. Gather a few people and start teaching them what you know. Giving value to people dramatically boosts your confidence. The more people you help, the more value you give and the more praise you get, which is very good for your confidence and esteem. Even if it is one person, just teach them what you know and feel good too.

Connect with Louistas

Your Notes! Your Symptoms!

Your feel-good file:

What, Who, makes you feel good?

....

....

....

....

....

....

....

....

Your family:

....

....

....

....

....

....

Connect with Louistas

Your friends:

....
....
....
....
....
....
....
....
....

Your hobbies

....
....
....
....
....
....
....
....

Connect with Louistas

Holidays

....
....
....
....
....
....
....
....
....

Job/career

....
....
....
....
....
....
....
....

[Connect with Louistas](#)

Nature/pets

Connect with Louistas

Connect with Louistas

Have Someone Else Weed Out The Negative "Stuff"

Is there something in your life right now that can ruin your entire day? Maybe it's getting an email from your child's teacher about lack of focus in class. Maybe it's a nasty comment left on your blog or an email from an irritated customer. Or maybe it's just some of the ridiculous things people will post on social media. If one little comment or email can send you down a spiral of self-doubt, it's time to weed out that negativity and if needed put a gate keeper in place.

Let's say you have a thriving online business, and you get plenty of notes from happy customers all week long. (Those are great things to stick into your "feel good" file btw.). But then you get that one nasty email from an enraged customer that ruins your entire day and makes you second guess everything you do. If that's you, find someone to filter the email for you. Hire a VA, get an intern, or simply have a spouse or friend deal with email for you. Have them handle it and only forward the good stuff to you.

Yes, if there's a serious issue, you are going to want to know about it. You can have your assistant do that... but

Connect with Louistas

The Success Mindset

if it's a simple matter of someone else having a bad day and letting it out on you, and your skin isn't thick enough to handle it… find someone else to deal with it to keep your own self-doubt at bay.

Your Notes! Your Symptoms!

Someone you know, like and trust! Give them a ring now!

....
....
....
....
....
....
....
....
....
....
....
....
....

Connect with Louistas

The Success Mindset

[Connect with Louistas](#)

The Success Mindset

Learn To Focus On The Good Stuff – Make It A Habit

Let's go back to the last example. I mentioned that sometimes we can have lots of great feedback (plenty of happy customers emailing us all week long for example), with only one bad egg in the bunch. And guess what we focus on? The negative. And we allow it to color everything else we've accomplished. That must stop!

Instead of always focusing on the negative, make it a habit to focus on the good stuff. It's not going to be easy and it's not something that comes natural to most of us, but with a little effort it can be done.

Every time you focus on the bad stuff, stop yourself and force yourself to focus on the good stuff instead. After a while it will become a habit… a habit that will boost your self-confidence and break the cycle of self-doubt.

When you focus on good and positive stuff, good and positive stuff happen to you. When you make it a habit, nature recognizes it and works with you by placing you in the right place, at the right time for growth opportunities. Yes! Some of these shall be negative. Use them positively. Note, that in every disappointment is an appointment.

Connect with Louistas

The Success Mindset

Your Notes! Your Symptoms!

Some positive stuff that you can always fall back to!

....

....

....

....

....

....

....

....

....

....

....

....

....

....

....

....

....

Connect with Louistas

Connect with Louistas

Stop Self Doubt In Its Tracks

This next tip is like the last one... but this time we're looking at the flip side. Learn to recognize when you start to doubt yourself. Whenever you start to second guess yourself or find yourself shying away from something new, different, or challenging, ask yourself if it's a case of self-doubt.

If so, start by validating the feeling. Yes, you are doubting yourself and you aren't feeling confident. Then start using one of the strategies I've shared with you already to stop it in its tracks right away. Just as being confident and doing stuff even when you're scared is a habit, giving in to self-doubt is a habit... in this case a bad habit. And it's time you start to break it. And you do that by recognizing it for what it is each time you can and then doing something about it. Keep at it and before you know it, your self-doubt will go down while your confidence in yourself and your abilities goes up.

When you are faced with making a decision, ask very clear questions to yourself – questions that the answer shall be a clear "yes" or "no". Then follow your heart's decision that shall lead to more confidence, growth, and success. In this way, self-doubt knows you don't play games.

Connect with Louistas

Your Notes! Your Symptoms!

Some positive activities that you can always do to feel good about yourself!

....

....

....

....

....

....

....

....

....

....

....

....

....

....

....

....

....

....

Connect with Louistas

[Connect with Louistas](#)

Keep A Journal

Keeping a journal is a great way to force yourself to reflect on what you're doing and what you have accomplished. What does this have to do with self-doubt? The journal will help you pinpoint cases when you're doubting yourself and allowing it to keep you from doing what you really want to do.

As you write about your day, you'll dig deeper and learn more about what's motivating your decisions. This alone can be helpful in pinpointing times when you start to doubt yourself.

What has worked very well for me is that I have eight major topics in my journal under which I arrange my day. I have physical goals, spiritual goals, psychological goals, financial goals, family goals, business goals, skills-based goals and nutrition goals. My to-do list for the day has at least a point under these seven points. From these, there are some that must be achieved on that day. I aim to accomplish these before midday. And at the end of the day, I evaluate and tick the boxes of the achieved goals. If the goal is not achieved, I condition myself to work on it until passed midnight before I can go to bed. In this way, my brain knows that it should not play tricks with me the

[Connect with Louistas](#)

next time I set a goal or plan an activity. I also go back often through the previous pages to check if there were items unticked that I need to work on. This ensures that I am achieving my goals. This adds to my confidence because I can see the success.

A journal gives you a chance to work through those challenges and mental blocks, but it also does something else. A journal is a personal record of what you're doing and who you are as a person. Even a quick little bullet journal entry reveals a lot about yourself. And more importantly it allows you to go back and discover how far you've come.

When you are starting to doubt yourself, or are trying to kick self-doubt to the curb, browse through your journals and take note of the progress you've made in the past weeks, months, and years. You'll realize that challenges are part of life and that there are plenty that seemed unsurmountable that you've tackled in the past. That will give you the confidence and the boost you need to work through your current doubts and fears.

Writing your goals and recording your achievements is a massive way of training your subconscious to feel good about yourself. This feeling can dramatically boost your confidence and eliminate self-doubt and low self-esteem.

Connect with Louistas

The Success Mindset

Your Notes! Your Symptoms!

Start journaling here:

Monday

....

....

....

....

....

....

....

....

Tuesday

....

....

....

....

....

....

....

[Connect with Louistas](#)

Wednesday

....

....

....

....

....

....

....

....

Thursday

....

....

....

....

....

....

....

....

Connect with Louistas

Friday

Saturday

Connect with Louistas

Sunday

[Connect with Louistas](#)

The Success Mindset

Connect with Louistas

Be Spontaneous In Taking Action

Have you taken the time to look back at some of your interests, hobbies, or ideas? Are there things you thought of doing and self-doubt convinced you not to look at for whatever reason. And now, the idea has become the most successful thing out there, done or executed by someone else? How do you feel when you see that new online course which you yourself could have written better? How do you feel when you hear that song which resembles your thoughts and lyrics, but you just never wrote it? How do you feel when that book with a similar content in your mind has just been published and yours is in your mind? Or what about returning to that unmade bed, dirty dishes, and untidy house – things you could spontaneously do almost in an automatic fashion.

The antidot to this feeling and mental reality is to practice being spontaneous. In relation to keeping a diary, when thought come to mind, write them down and execute them immediately. When you think of an action, just do it. When people ask you a question, just give the answer that comes out first – never say I do not know – if you do not genuinely know, suggest where they could find the answer. By this you are training your mind to act

Connect with Louistas

spontaneously. By so doing you banish self-doubt and encourage your subconscious to always think action and not postponement.

Your Notes! Your Symptoms!

Where do you hesitate most and how will you next react?

………………………………………………………………………………………

………………………………………………………………………………………

………………………………………………………………………………………

………………………………………………………………………………………

………………………………………………………………………………………

………………………………………………………………………………………

………………………………………………………………………………………

………………………………………………………………………………………

………………………………………………………………………………………

………………………………………………………………………………………

………………………………………………………………………………………

………………………………………………………………………………………

Connect with Louistas

[Connect with Louistas](#)

Get Better At What You Do

Sometimes our self-doubt is justified. Yet, often, it's not, but sometimes it is. When that's the case, it's time to buckle down and get the education, experience, tools, advice, or information you need to take the next step.

Have you attended an interview and they said you were very good, but the job was not yours yet? Study the reasons why and go back with more force. Have you attempted to start a relationship with someone you think you have fallen in love with and have been rejected? Take lessons on how to approach people and always get a yes! Have you been waiting for that job promotion, and it is not coming? Improve your talents and showcase them – be resourceful. Have you practiced your skills for a long time, and you know you have a lot to offer others, yet doubt yourself? Start teaching people about your skills. The more you teach, the more you research and grow, and the more your confidence grows.

Go sign up for a class, talk to a mentor, volunteer ... do whatever it takes to get better at what you do. With that knowledge and experience under your belt, you're ready for the next chapter in your life, your profession, or your hobby. T. Robbins talks about *"Raising Your Standards"*.

Connect with Louistas

The Success Mindset

Your Notes! Your Symptoms!

What practical steps shall you take?

Choose three areas of life to start with.

Area 1.

....
....
....
....
....
....
....
....
....
....
....
....
....
....
....

Connect with Louistas

Area 2

....
....
....
....
....
....
....
....
....

Area 3.

....
....
....
....
....
....
....
....

Connect with Louistas

The Success Mindset

Connect with Louistas

The Success Mindset

Don't Let Temporary Setbacks or Distractions Hold You Back

Setbacks are going to happen... let's just get real about that. And so will distractions. Life likes to throw curveballs and there isn't anything we can do about. But we do have control about how we react to temporary setbacks and distractions.

The first thing I want you to realize is that they are just that – temporary. Hence, we have to change the way we think about the situation. Acknowledge them and then move on. This begins to form a habit and will remind you the next time you encounter a similar setback to Keep going without allowing them to fuel your self-doubt. Instead, use it as a challenge to push harder and go further. Remember, reasons don't count, but results do matter. Pursue the results and challenge the reasons.

Someone once told me that when life gives you lemons, do not bite them and complain that they are sour. Instead use the lemons to make lemonade. Its also a known fact that people who fail in life do so because they tried something. If you do not try, you cannot fail. And when you get setbacks in what you have tried to do, use them as springboards for further success.

Connect with Louistas

The Success Mindset

Your Notes! Your Symptoms!

What are your goals?

....
....
....
....
....
....
....
....
....
....
....
....
....
....
....
....
....
....

Connect with Louistas

The Success Mindset

What is stopping you from achieving them?

....

....

....

....

....

....

....

....

....

....

....

....

....

....

....

....

....

....

....

[Connect with Louistas](#)

Connect with Louistas

Remember - Nothing Is Permanent

Finally, remember that nothing is permanent. When you're worried about failing and allowing that fear to stop you from doing what you love, think back to the tip about imagining "what's the worst that can happen". Then remember that no matter how bad that may be – feeling rejected, failing, being ridiculed – it is not permanent and it's something you can completely overcome.

I used to think that I was incapable of making money online until I made my first £100. I used to think that you could only love one person at a time, but there is enough love to give to the whole world. We believed that the "world" was flat, that there were nine planets – guess what we now know about galaxies. It was nighttime yesterday and it is daytime today – nothing is permanent. So why make your situational self-doubt permanent?

Yes, you will make mistakes. But that's ok… it is how we learn and how we get better. Fail fast and fail often to become good at whatever you want to do. And those failures and setbacks aren't permanent.

When you think about it that way, there really is no reason not to give whatever it is you want to do a try.

Connect with Louistas

Your Notes! Your Symptoms!

What are some of the obstacles you have overcome in the past? How did you do it?

....

....

....

....

....

....

....

....

....

....

....

....

....

....

....

....

....

Connect with Louistas

Connect with Louistas

The Success Mindset

Connect with Louistas

Chapter 4

Further Tips and articles on how to multiply your self-confidence

You can do all things

if you truly believe you can!

Connect with Louistas

How to Raise Your Self-Esteem Through Self-Talk

Your self-esteem level can be precarious. It can go up or down at any point depending on such situational things like whether you're late to work, how your day is progressing, or what your boss just said to you. In a minute you can be on top of the world and the next minute down to the depths of self-doubt. It's no wonder therefore that your self-esteem must be nurtured, but sometimes it's hard to figure out how to do it in a way that's best for you. Self-talk is the answer!

What you say to yourself can make the difference between success and failure. Unfortunately, people tend to be their own worst critics. This just means that you're more likely to be much harder on yourself for making a mistake than you would be for a family member or even a stranger. This doesn't have to be the way you treat yourself. When you talk to yourself, say something you want to hear! Encourage and congratulate yourself even for the little things. When your self-talk is positive, your self-esteem can soar, and you can maintain a healthy self-esteem through anything life can throw at you.

Connect with Louistas

Eliminate The Negative

The first thing you'll want to do is analyse your current self-talk patterns. What are you saying to yourself? The story you tell yourself each day about you is the same story you are acting out, whether you are fully aware or not. People can also see through, even if you are able to pretend.

Identify the instances where you're negative. You might be telling yourself that you can't accomplish something. You may be beating yourself up because you made a mistake. Or you may just be generally discouraging with yourself and developing lazy habits. Those negative patterns should be wake up calls for you to start talking courageously and positively to yourself with tender loving care.

To raise your self-esteem, you must first erase your negative self-talk. Give yourself the benefit of the doubt and start treating yourself with understanding. If you feel like you haven't accomplished enough, shift your focus over to what you have accomplished. At the end of the day, you'll begin to feel proud of yourself instead of discouraged. It's just one step closer to being happy and comfortable with who you are!

Connect with Louistas

Be Positive

After you've identified where you've been negative in your life, you can concentrate on the real positive aspects. As we have mentioned earlier, you should focus on the good, positive, and successful stuff. You have opportunities all the time to treat yourself right, and you can take advantage of them with the help of positive self-talk.

Consider the following tips:

1. **Congratulate yourself.** When you've done a job well, take the time to congratulate yourself. It's important to give yourself a pat on the back every now and then. Even if you haven't accomplished anything huge, you're certainly making progress. Reflect on how good it makes you feel. Then add something into that positive memory diary.

2. **Use affirmations.** One way to bring positive energy into your life is to use positive affirmations. Affirmations are short positive statements that are written in the present tense. Say them to yourself often as a reminder of what a great person you are (because you are!). Look at yourself in the mirror

Connect with Louistas

The Success Mindset

and say to that person in the mirror "I love you". Affirm to yourself that you are successful; that you are hardworking; that you are progressively getting better at what you do. Affirmations have such a powerful ability to influence the mind and hence you should take advantage and practice them every day

3. **Believe in yourself.** Someone else can tell you that you're good enough to accomplish anything, but it'll never make a difference if you don't believe it yourself. It's the motivation and belief in yourself that will always pick you back up when you fall. Remember, the story you tell yourself is the same story you are acting out. Everyone deals with failure from time to time but remember that it's a learning experience too. Maybe you'll learn something during a "failure" that gives you the knowledge to finally succeed. Consider it a gift in disguise! When you take the time to be positive and patient with yourself every day, you'll raise your self-esteem. Allow yourself to be human, focus on the positive, and you'll go far.

Connect with Louistas

The Success Mindset

Your Notes! Your Symptoms!

What are some successes you have achieved? Recognise and affirm them.

How did you do it?

....

....

....

....

....

....

....

....

....

....

....

....

....

....

....

[Connect with Louistas](#)

[Connect with Louistas](#)

I Am Free Of Self-Doubt – 2 Affirmations.

I am brimming with confidence. I deserve to have a high level of self-confidence. Self-doubt is a foreign concept to me. All I know is confidence. As my confidence grows, the room available for self-doubt disappears.

Even when others feel anxious and filled with worry, **I am free of self-doubt**. I can maintain my confidence even when around others that are concerned.

I am independent of my environment. **I choose how I feel, and I choose to feel confident.** I expect positive outcomes. I am an optimist.

I trust myself. I am impressed with my ability to handle any situation with wisdom and creativity.

I know how to be successful. I have proven this to myself numerous times. **When I reflect on my accomplishments, my confidence in myself grows.** I learn from my failures, so failing ultimately builds my self-confidence, too.

I make decisions quickly. I take decisive action. **The trust and confidence I have in myself are comforting.**

Connect with Louistas

Each successful day I live brings even greater certainty. **I am more confident** today than I was yesterday. I know I can be even more confident tomorrow.

Today, **I am living confidently and free of self-doubt.** I am putting my plans into action and believe that everything is working out for the best. I am free of self-doubt.

I leave the past in the past and focus on the future.

I am able to **stay focused on the present and the future**. My ability to avoid dwelling on the past is increasing. I understand that thinking about the past has negative consequences.

There is nothing left for me in the past but lessons. That is the good thing about the past – the lessons it provides. I take those lessons and apply them to my present. Focusing on the past, though, leads to regret.

I choose to look forward. **I spend five minutes each day to imagine the future** I wish to experience. I know that a compelling future is the best way to stay motivated and positive.

I work hard in the present to create my future. I can only interact with time in the present moment. I make the most of each moment and look forward to enjoying the future even more.

[Connect with Louistas](#)

The Success Mindset

Your Notes! Your Symptoms!

What are some successes you have achieved? Recognise and affirm them.

....

....

....

....

....

....

....

....

....

....

....

....

....

....

....

....

....

Connect with Louistas

Chapter 5

How to Overcome Self-Doubt When Presenting Your Ideas to Peers

Everyone starts from somewhere,

probably as scared as you are!

Connect with Louistas

As unbelievable as it sounds, it's the norm for many people to doubt themselves. So, if you have feelings of self-doubt, you're in good company as we have already seen!

Doubting yourself creates a host of unfavorable scenarios and prevents you from living up to your full potential. It holds you back. Many opportunities pass you by because you feel like you're lacking in some way.

Self-doubt is especially prevalent in the presence of peers. It's easy for others on your level academically or professionally to challenge your self-belief – just by being there! You might feel like they're ahead, even though you're on the same level. It's important to realize that you're just as deserving as anybody else.

Keeping these concepts in mind will help you feel confident in the presence of peers:

You Did The Work.

Take a moment and remind yourself about how much work you've done and how much effort it has taken to get to where you are. And then believe that you have done a good job in the preparation.

[Connect with Louistas](#)

Whether it's getting through school or putting in years as a junior staff member, you've done it yourself. You've worked your way in, and to the middle, or the top. Think back to all the obstacles you had to overcome to reach where you are today. They all matter. They all added up to this. You have done well and enough.

It wasn't easy, but it was worth it. And that's why you're worth every success that comes your way! Avoid shortchanging the work you put in.

You've Been Validated.

The people at the top have validated you. They've told you that the work you put in qualifies you for your current status. Why are you questioning that? Your age also suggests that you have been around in this planet for a few years and knows something more. Even nature and the ground on which you stand has validated you.

If you have a college degree, then the experts in your area of study have confirmed that you're knowledgeable in your field. Your degree shows that you're good at what you do, and you can walk through life with confidence in that field.

[Connect with Louistas](#)

Perhaps you received a promotion at work. Your boss acknowledged the quality of your work and rewarded you. Embrace the opportunity and feel a bit taller!

Your Track Record Speaks For Itself.

Look back and assess the path you've taken and the successes you've had along the way. You probably have an impressive track record. Now if only you could see it! Remember that earlier we talked about keeping a positive memories diary – use it to remind you of your positive and successful record.

Consider how many people after you may benefit from your achievements. That's nothing to take lightly! You're a game-changer, even if you don't realize it. Consider how many people may like to be where you are at now but can't. You have an advantage over many people and should feel courageous with your peers because you are worth it.

And consider this! By reading this book and grasping these concepts, you have doubled your value because you shall become a more confident expert in your field. Add this into your personal development CV column.

[Connect with Louistas](#)

You're Deserving Of Goodness.

That spotlight is just as much yours as it is anybody else's. We're all created equal from the perspective of human existence. So, embrace all the good things that are yours.

Use some of the time you spend praising others to praise yourself. This is a challenge and I like you to take it on – to stand in front of the mirror, look at yourself and say, "congratulations me". And when you achieve a goal by the end of the day, say to yourself, "Well done!" If no one says it to you, say it to yourself – your brain loves conversing with you. That is how you build character – by convincing your brains of the character you want to be.

Avoid feeling guilty about speaking up for yourself. Your voice ought to be heard. You're validated by your experience, expertise, and education. Improve your self-confidence and shine.

Today's the day. Open your window and toss self-doubt out of your life. You'll realize how quickly new opportunities present themselves when you make room for them. Take control and show your peers that you're just as worthy as they are. When they talk negatively, speak positively. When they talk failure, speak about success. When they swear, praise instead. Be good!

[Connect with Louistas](#)

Your Notes! Your Symptoms!

What are your credentials that have qualified you to do this presentation, this job, or this career?

Keep them in mind when you are faced with a bit of doubt in your abilities.

....

....

....

....

....

....

....

....

....

....

....

....

....

....

Connect with Louistas

[Connect with Louistas](#)

The Success Mindset

[Connect with Louistas](#)

Chapter 6

Self-Assertiveness Strategies to Help You Reclaim Your Domain

Assertiveness is the force that propels the engines of discipline and success!

Connect with Louistas

As you seek success in your business, love life, or any other venture, it helps to take stock of your level of self-assertiveness. Assertiveness is the ability to honestly express yourself without undue self-doubt or anxiety. If others think they can walk all over you, they tend to view you in a negative light. While some are born assertive, for others self-assertiveness is a cultivated skill.

Learn how to become more self-assertive by following these steps:

Becoming more assertive may not be a day's job. It needs great conviction, dedication and commitment from your whole being to succeed. As you shall see, you need small building block and goals to see you through. And once you are there, you gain a certain confidence, respect and honour that is beautiful to behold. Go on and practice these.

Identify Your Boundaries.

The very first step to mastering self-assertiveness is figuring out where to draw the line. How much abuse are you willing to take?

Connect with Louistas

Be honest with yourself and avoid letting self-doubt stop you from defining new boundaries.

Start by writing down where you draw the line in various situations and pay attention to your internal reactions. Recall past situations in which you let someone go too far. How did you feel? At what point could you have put your foot down?

Research has shown that when you externalize your thought process by writing things down, you'll have a better chance of making a lasting impact on your future behaviour.

Forgive Wisely.

Although the ability to forgive is important for your well-being, it's possible to go too far. If you continually forgive someone for their bad behaviour, they're more likely to offend again. Parasitic personalities, when they realize they can hurt you with impunity, will do so.

One way you can empower yourself is to cut ties with the toxic individuals in your life. While the split may be painful initially, you'll likely blossom once you're free of their influence.

[Connect with Louistas](#)

With your newfound improved self-esteem and confidence, you'll attract individuals who will treat you with the respect you deserve.

Think Strategically.

As you build up your self-assertiveness, you'll need a strategy to deal with individuals who overstep your boundaries.

Assertiveness requires a clear and calm discourse, rather than a verbal shouting match. Generally, the calmer you are when you engage the offender, the more effective your conversation will be.

Even extremely intelligent people can be totally ignorant about how their behaviour affects others. This isn't meant to give these individuals an excuse. However, it's possible that if you haven't asserted yourself previously, the person overstepping their bounds may be unaware of how their behaviour comes across.

The Unofficial acronym ASSAP represents an effective strategy to keep the conversation on topic and to the point:

Connect with Louistas

- **A**lert the person that you would like to speak with them.
- **S**tate your grievance clearly and calmly – from your perspective.
- **S**ell the benefits of them altering their behaviour.
- **A**gree that they'll do things differently in the future.
- **P**raise them for something they've done well – even agreeing to listen.

If you find yourself slipping at any point, bring yourself back to the last main point of the conversation before it veered.

Always Remain Calm.

You may find that when you confront someone about their behaviour, they become defensive. ***Do your best to remain calm.***

The individual may feel as if they're under attack, especially if you haven't taken them to task before. In this situation, your opponent will likely try to derail you by changing the subject. Avoid allowing this to happen. Remember you have a duty, a responsibility, and a point to pass across.

[Connect with Louistas](#)

Use Honesty As A Tool.

Honesty is essential to healthy relationships, and you can use it as a tool to reinforce your boundaries.

Set clear boundaries and let others know that you're not a pushover. You'll likely find that becoming assertive will change your life. Once you've reclaimed your power, avoid letting anyone encroach on your domain ever again.

However, be generous with your honesty and some honesty, which destroys other people, may also destroy all that you have been building. Think, win-win honesty.

Keep To Your Word.

Let your "yes" be a "yes" and let your "no" be your "no". If you have worked on the principles above for a long time, you shall trust your judgement. And hence your decisions shall be informed by true and certain conscience, correct and positive principles. A person that does not weaver from their thoughts is stronger than the person who changes their mind easily.

However, the person who also realises that they made a poor decision and change their "Yes" or "No", based on the evidence available, is also as noble and confident.

Connect with Louistas

The Success Mindset

Your Notes! Your Symptoms!

What are your assertive qualities right now – what level are you at?

....

....

....

....

....

....

....

....

....

....

....

....

....

....

....

....

....

Connect with Louistas

What boundaries will you like to set?

………………………………………………………………………………………………
………………………………………………………………………………………………
………………………………………………………………………………………………
………………………………………………………………………………………………
………………………………………………………………………………………………
………………………………………………………………………………………………
………………………………………………………………………………………………
………………………………………………………………………………………………
………………………………………………………………………………………………

Who deserves your forgiveness?

………………………………………………………………………………………………
………………………………………………………………………………………………
………………………………………………………………………………………………
………………………………………………………………………………………………
………………………………………………………………………………………………
………………………………………………………………………………………………
………………………………………………………………………………………………
………………………………………………………………………………………………

[Connect with Louistas](#)

What thinking strategies do you need to develop?

……………………………………………………………………………………

……………………………………………………………………………………

……………………………………………………………………………………

……………………………………………………………………………………

……………………………………………………………………………………

……………………………………………………………………………………

……………………………………………………………………………………

……………………………………………………………………………………

How is your emotional intelligence – what do you need to work on most?

……………………………………………………………………………………

……………………………………………………………………………………

……………………………………………………………………………………

……………………………………………………………………………………

……………………………………………………………………………………

……………………………………………………………………………………

……………………………………………………………………………………

……………………………………………………………………………………

[Connect with Louistas](#)

The Success Mindset

How honest are you to yourself and others?

[Connect with Louistas](#)

Connect with Louistas

The Success Mindset

Connect with Louistas

Chapter 7

I can, I will, I must be confident

"If you think you can, you can! If you think you can't, you probably can't

(Les .Brown, 2020)

Connect with Louistas

Daily, you have to believe, convince yourself and practice confidence thoughts in order to build the confidence fibers in your brain.

The "I Can" Checklist

Use this checklist as a reminder of the important steps you can take to develop an "I Can" attitude. You'll soon discover that you've become action-oriented, saying "I Can" instead of "I Can't!"

Combating Self-Doubt

_____ Don't take criticism personally.

_____ Find ways to improve your skills.

_____ Think about past successes.

_____ Break the problem or task into manageable pieces.

_____ Delegate what you can.

Connect with Louistas

Changing The Negative Mindset

_____ Pull out your action plan and examine your goals.

_____ Examine your strategy for achieving those goals.

_____ Decide how to get what your life is lacking.

_____ Make new goals to get what you want.

_____ Divide your goals into achievable steps.

_____ Establish support groups and lean on them when necessary.

Finding Your Positive Attitude

_____ Be thankful.

_____ Be flexible.

_____ Journal your thoughts.

_____ Use personal mantras or positive affirmations daily.

Connect with Louistas

[Connect with Louistas](#)

8 Activities That Build Your Self-Confidence

Everything becomes easier when you're brimming with self-confidence. *As soon as self-doubt enters your mind, your ability to act is compromised.* Self-confidence might seem to rise and fall in a random fashion, but there are steps you can take to increase the level of confidence you experience on a regular basis.

Enhance your self-confidence and accomplish more with these techniques:

1. **Achieve a goal.** Start small. Your goal might be to arrive to work on time every day this week or to eat a piece of fruit each day. Easy goals are easy to accomplish. When you accomplish something, you feel more confident. *Choose easy goals that make a difference.* The accomplishment of many, small goals will change your level of confidence.

2. **Make a list of your accomplishments.** It's interesting that our failures are easy to list, but our accomplishments require a little more pondering. Make a list of your accomplishments and review them each day. Remember how great you felt in that moment.

[Connect with Louistas](#)

3. **Groom yourself to a higher standard.** Get a better haircut. Spend a little more time and attention on your grooming each morning. Learn how to apply your makeup more effectively. Trim your beard in a more attractive manner. Trim those stray ear and nose hairs. You'll be surprised how much better you look and feel.

4. **Be assertive.** As mentioned earlier, ***Having more control over your life results in greater self-confidence.*** One of the quickest ways to increase the level of influence you have over your life is to be more assertive. Give yourself small tasks to accomplish that require assertiveness. A few examples you might consider:

    - Walk into a fast-food restaurant and ask for a cup of water without ordering anything else. It doesn't matter whether your request is granted. Just ask.

    - Tell your boss one thing you'd like to change about your job or your work environment.

[Connect with Louistas](#)

The Success Mindset

- Make one suggestion to your significant other that would enhance your relationship.

5. **Dress nicer.** We all feel more confident when we're dressed well. Up your game and put the "nice clothes" in your closet to work for you. Think of your friend or co-worker that dresses the best. Shoot for a similar level of clothing while maintaining your own style. It takes the same amount of time to put on a nicer shirt.

6. **Practice.** *Practice breeds confidence.* You'll be much more confident if you practice your speech ten times instead of five. Whether you practice your flirting skills, or your ability give presentations, your confidence will increase with practice.

7. **Drop one thing from your life.** The odds are high that you're currently stuck with an obligation in your life that you don't enjoy. While there are some things in life you must do, there are just as many that you don't. ***Take control and drop one of these non-essential activities that you prefer not to do anyway.***

Connect with Louistas

8. **Find a mentor.** The right mentor can make all the difference. Knowing that you have an expert on your side is sure to boost your confidence. A good mentor will provide the support and guidance necessary to reach your goals. Good mentors aren't easy to find, but well worth the effort to locate. Take your time to look for a mentor who will provide most of what you need.

Some of us are blessed with a high level of self-confidence while others must learn to cultivate it. *Focus on your accomplishments, be more assertive, and find a mentor.* Spend time each day growing your self-confidence and experience real personal growth.

Short Affirmation

I achieve my goals that I set daily. My eyes are focused on them, and nothing shall derail me.

My list of accomplished goals is a testament and proof of my success and high standards I have set.

Today, I am clean, assertive, focused, and modeling myself to great minds that I look up to.

Connect with Louistas

The Success Mindset

Your Notes! Your Symptoms!

What is your plan for achieving the 8 strategies? Provide details below!

....

....

....

....

....

....

....

....

....

....

....

....

....

....

....

....

....

....

[Connect with Louistas](#)

[Connect with Louistas](#)

I Am Free To Create My Own Reality.

I have choices in all situations. Nothing stands between me and my highest good. I have only to claim it, and it is mine!

Being in the flow of my creative power each day is my birthright, so I am free to shape my own reality.

I trust myself to make good choices. This includes choices about my perspectives and responses. Life situations come and go, but my positivity about them is unwavering. In this way among many ways, I create my reality. At my very best, I see myself as a positive person. This highest vision of myself is manifest in each moment.

When I set my heart and mind on something, I trust that it is even now coming to pass. I know that I have infinite co-creative power in my own life. Whatever I want my reality to look like, I manifest in abundance. I am secure in my right to my own happiness.

When a situation turns out in a way other than how I desire, I know that something better is in its place. I am confident in this because I am constantly creating my reality and my reality is good!

[Connect with Louistas](#)

The Success Mindset

My perspective on situations is always in my control, so I choose happiness and joy for myself.

Today, I am confident in my own co-creative power. And I use my abilities wisely. I am free to create my own reality, so in each moment I choose to create it in my highest good.

Self-Reflection Questions:

1. In the past year, have I successfully created a perspective that I wanted to have on a situation?
2. To me, what is the relationship between creativity and joy, bliss, or freedom?
3. How do I feel when I choose to shape my reality in a way that satisfies me?

Connect with Louistas

The Success Mindset

Your Notes! Your Symptoms!

What concrete actions shall you take each day to abandon the past and embrace the present and the future?

....

....

....

....

....

....

....

....

....

....

....

....

....

....

....

....

Connect with Louistas

Eliminating Self-Doubt Framework:

Throughout these pages, you have **been conceiving ideas** – remember that nothing has yet to exist when it was never conceived. Therefore, if you want to create your new self or improve your old ways, you have got to conceive of it – and that is what we hopefully have assisted you to do.

You have been **creating thoughts and concepts** in your mind. By going through the exercises, writing them down, and memorising them you were creating a new person; you were repairing and creating new nerons in your brain. The newly created cell however, do need to be kept active and alive.

You were constantly through reflection of the ideas, downloading them into your subconscious, **and experiencing them.** You would have chosen to experience them at a superficial or deeper level. The more your reflected on the ideas and concepts with emotions, enthusiam and belief, the more they were engraved in your subconscious, ready to do your will.

After every section, you were given tasks to do. You were given exercises and questions to complete. By completing these you **were taking the action** needed to lift you out

Connect with Louistas

of your previous or current state, into the desired, confident and successful you. Of course we hoped that you were doing the exercises as doing them was preparing to be successful.

Throughout the whole process of building your new self you were constantly using your **senses of memory and remembering.** Ther is nothing you could have concieved of, created, and experienced that was not primarily there. You just had to re-member them. And the more your remembered, the more your subconscious gained the power to form new paradigms for you.

The **transformations** should be less than remarkable if you have followed these stages. It is not a one time event but a life long process, which demands daily practice. If you have been transformed, remember you have just started.

But this is not the end, it is the beginning or continuation. Remember that if you start a journey and leave it half way, you will never arrive. And even if you finish the journey and still have to return home, you still have another journey ahead of you. That is why we have more courses for you in *"The Success Mindset Series"*. Check it out and use the accompanying workbooks to improve your mindset and grow beyon bounds.

Connect with Louistas

The Success Mindset

The Success Mindset: Eliminating Self Doubt.

Through no fault of ours, we are given a code after birth - self-doubt or low self-esteem.
But now you have the code to rewire your mindset and download a new courage code. You choose!

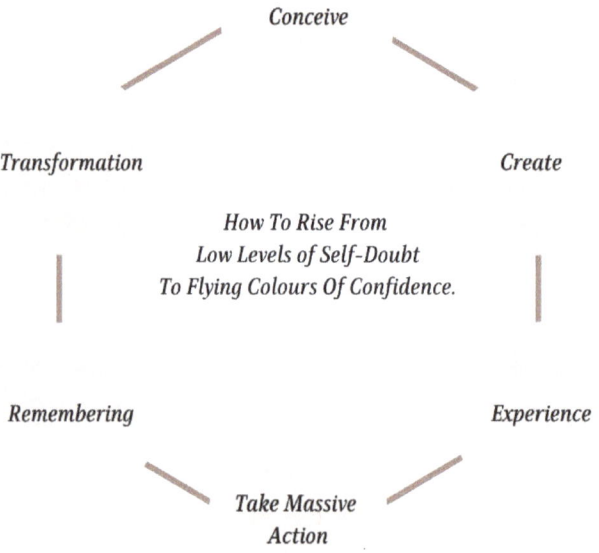

How To Rise From
Low Levels of Self-Doubt
To Flying Colours Of Confidence.

[Connect with Louistas](#)

The Success Mindset

Your Notes! Your Symptoms!

Write concrete actions for the implementation of the Framework here? Which part of the framework are you going to focus on more?

....

....

....

....

....

....

....

....

....

....

....

....

....

....

....

....

Connect with Louistas

[Connect with Louistas](#)

Conclusion:

I hope you have found this short book helpful. We've talked about what self-doubt is, what causes it and how it can affect every single aspect of your life. The lesson I hope you're taking away from those chapters is that self-doubt can be a distractive force in your life that you need to reign in on a regular basis.

And to do that, we focused on several different strategies in the last chapter. Remember the first four will work universally and are where you should start. Then move through the rest, starting with the tips and strategies that speak to you the most.

The key and what I want you to take away from this is to pay attention to your feelings, particularly self-doubt and fear, recognize them for what they are and then do whatever you have to do to reign them in and not allow them to control your life and what you want to do.

The great news is that the more you practice, the better you get at defeating self-doubt. The more action you take, the more conscious your subconscious builds your action potential. When you convince yourself that you can, and move on to do things, the easier it gets at believing in yourself and taking spontaneous actions. The

Connect with Louistas

more you build the confidence to try new things… which in turn builds more confidence, the more you participate in your own rescue. And before you know you're creating a self-propelling cycle of personal success that will make you unstoppable … and more importantly allow you to live a happy, fulfilled, and successful life.

Stay blessed!

Brighten your corner with joy!

Take massive action because you can,

you will,

and you must develop

The Success Mindset.

Connect with Louistas

The Success Mindset

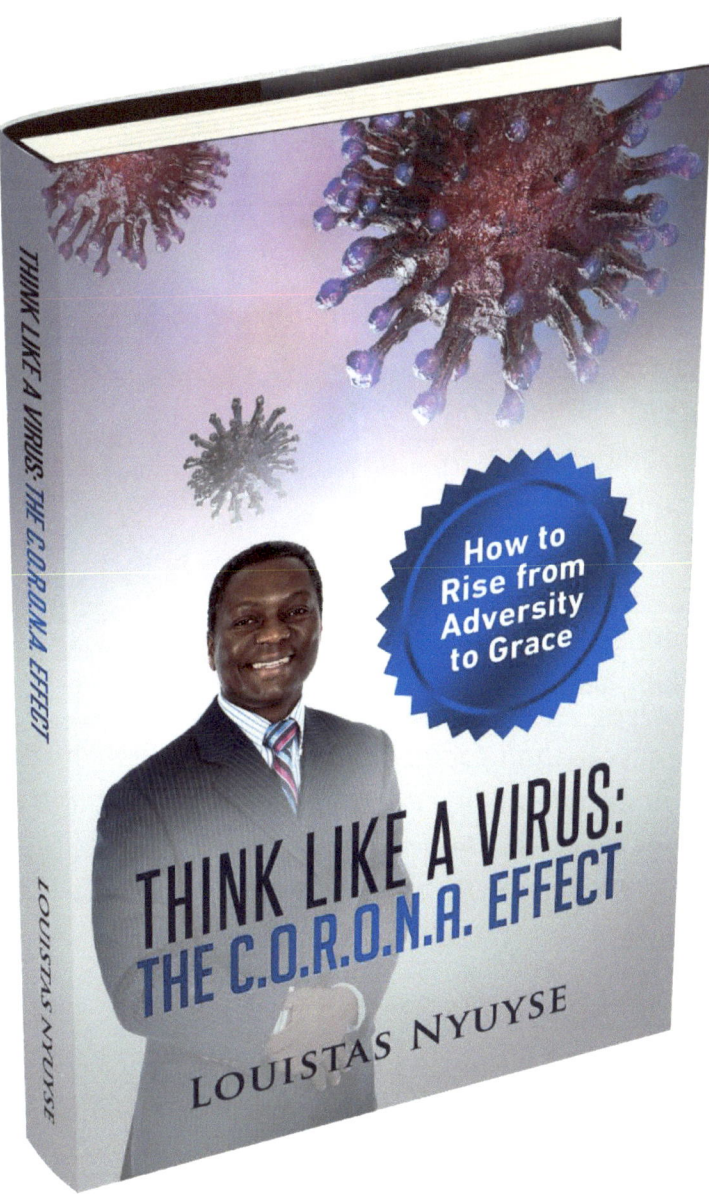

Connect with Louistas

Coming soon!

THE SUCCESS MINDSET SERIES:

The primary objective of this book was to share with your some of the lessons I have learnt while overcoming the many challenges I have faced in life. If you could just be a bit more confident in seeking knowledge, asking questions, and being resourceful; believing in your abilities, following your childhood passions, and taking action right now, you could improve your mindset and succeed in anything you do.

However, you shall face challenges. But what matters is what you do when they come. I hope that through these few pages, you have learnt one or two strategies that can help you face your challenges with hope, clarity, and confidence.

The Success Mindset: Eliminating Self-doubt has been written to be an ultimate practical tool and guide for you when you encounter self-doubt, low self-esteem, or low confidence.

If you think and feel that you do not know much; that you

[Connect with Louistas](#)

do not know what to expect; and that you constantly feel you can't do things, don't worry, the answers are within these pages. If you are full of fear to do things or progress, if you think you are not good enough at anything and feels like your past is always keeping you in the same position, then the solutions are right in here.

Practical steps like fear and do it anyway; taking baby steps; celebrating small successes; focusing on who you are helping; having someone weed out the negatives; being a spontaneous action taker; keeping a journal and many more, are strategies suggested in this book to help you grow in confidence, relationships, and wealth.

Connect with Louistas Nyuyse on social media for daily tips, strategies, and ideas to inspire you at https://bit.lyLouistas

[Connect with Louistas](#)

The Success Mindset

[Connect with Louistas](#)